My Journey as A Servant

Pastor Paulette Brockington

TRUE PERSPECTIVE
PUBLISHING HOUSE

Published in the United States of America
ISBN # 978-1-7350275-7-9

Special Thanks

We want to give God all the Glory, for what He has done. I personally thank my family, my husband Deacon Roosevelt Brockington, Sr., my children Rosalind, Paulette, Robert Brockington, my grandchildren. A special thanks to Reverend Brenda Avery who has been with me through thick and thin. She has been with me every step of the way in my journey from servant to leadership. Even through the litigations and court proceedings she has been steadfast, dependable, unmovable, and has been a true friend. A special thanks to Deacon Arlester Ellis who is a special friend. A special thanks to LaKeisha Strothers and her children for assisting me with whatever I needed, and not having any reservations or questions in helping me. Lastly a special thanks to Deaconess Rose Stinson who's faithful to me in whatever I do.

A special thanks to the following persons who have been an inspiration to me:

·   Bishop Mary Jackson

·   Pastor Karen Rutherford

·   Bishop Linward Bush

·   Overseer John McClure

·   Mother Ruberstein McClure

·   Apostle Barbara Vaughn

·   Apostle Derrick L. Wells

·   Bishop William Young, Jr.

·   Phadra Hanks

·   Denise K. Brockington

·   Louise Coleman

Acknowledgments

To Dr. Ida M. Simpson who taught me to be a lady, a wife, and a mother.

To Bishop John L. Taylor for being a spiritual leader, a father figure, and all around good friend; also to his wife Overseer Linda Taylor.

Contents

Forward... vi

Dedication...….. vii

Introduction….. viii

Chapter 1- The Founder: Bishop Jessie Ford, Jr.
Story His Biography and the Church
History…...…... 10

Chapter 2- The Legacy of Sallie A. Bruce............ 13

Chapter 3 - The Servant Becomes the Leader
(The Mantle Has Been Passed Down)................. 21

Chapter 4 – When the Servant Leader
Bleeds a Time of Reflection.......................…... 25

Chapter 5 -The Bonus Chapter the
Announcer Speaks.. 29

Conclusion... 50

A Pictorial of Servitude................................. 55

Pastor Paulette Brockington
Affirmation Word Collage............................. 106

Foreword

Welcome to the journey of Pastor Paulette Brockington. This book will enlighten readers to the road traveled that has bought her to where she is today.

While reading about her journey this book will show her dedication, loyalty, and commitment to being a servant and evolving into a leader. Her story will show how God in His infinite wisdom, strength, and power guided her through the good, the bad, losses, and ultimately the successes in becoming a strong leader. Great leaders are not born, they are made according to the scripture Proverbs 27:17, **"Iron Sharpens iron…"**.

This story is about a woman who was a dedicated servant for twenty-eight years and how God moved her into leadership because she remained faithful, obedient, and committed. She accomplished the highest calling from God, and that is successfully leading His people to understand the importance of servitude and cultivating a personal relationship with God.

The role from a servant to the role of a leader isn't linear, but there were many hard times, trials, and tribulations along the way. Her faith was tested, her patience tried, and her love put to the test. But it was God's voice that ultimately pushed her to stay the course, and she was determined not to be defeated. This book will show the honesty, grit, and determination of how Pastor Paulette Brockington came from a servant to the rise of leadership.

This is a book of truth, a story of a journey of how a servant became the Shero for God's people!

-Mary M. Walker

Dedications

To my husband, Roosevelt Brockington Sr. for allowing me to serve and support Pastor Bruce for 28 years.

To my family for the sacrifices they made concerning my having to be away so much.

To the memory of the late Overseer Sallie A. Bruce for her Pastorship, leadership, love, faithfulness, and no-nonsense teaching.

To the memory of Anthony Bruce who passed away on November 25, 1997 he was my #1 aficionado.

To the memory of my late son Roosevelt Brockington, Jr. passed away on January 01, 2011.

To the memory of the late Bishop Robert Simpson Jr. who gave me the opportunity to assist Pastor Sallie Bruce at the St. John Church of God.

This book is dedicated to every member that is under my leadership.

Introduction

It is time for the announcer to speak! In order for me to tell "my story", I have to begin with the stories of the Founder, the late Bishop Jessie Ford Jr., and his successor the then minister, turned pastor, and later Overseer Sallie A. Bruce. This story will chronicle the history and events of the St. John Church of God by Bishop Ford's accounts, then his death and the induction of Sallie A. Bruce as the chosen one to become pastor of this great church.

Pastor Sallie A. Bruce served as pastor and leader for 28 years and I, being her faithful servant in Christ, stood by her side as she suffered these lengthy life changing illnesses. Eventually she succumbed to the complications of pre-existing health conditions and a stroke which led to her death in 2013.

Before she passed away, through Pastor Bruce, the Lord led her to pass the mantle to me as the third predecessor of the St. John Church of God. Thus my journey and induction from servant to pastor began. Because I had been a faithful and willing servant, doing the work of the Lord in serving my pastor Dr. Sallie A. Bruce, the Lord saw fit for me to serve His people in the highest form; leadership.

For many years I was a servant, announcer, and forerunner for this great woman of God. God has not only used my voice to cry aloud and spare not, but I've been the assistant Pastor for many years. Working alongside and taking just as many stripes as the anointed Dr. Sallie A. Bruce. I've been her eyes, her ears, her legs, and most importantly her voice! In order to be a great leader, one must learn the art of being a great follower.

Continue reading this amazing story of how three leaders were destined to be entwined to build upon God's great Kingdom. I am Pastor Paulette Brockington and….

The Announcer Speaks!

Chapter One

The Beginning:

The Founder Bishop Jessie Ford, Jr's. Story

His Biography and the Church History

Jessie Ford, Jr. had given his life to the Lord at age 16 he was saved, sanctified and filled with the Holy Ghost under the leadership of the late W.E. Fuller, Jr. The young Jessie Ford preached his trial sermon on April 7, 1953. He served as the church's janitor, later he was promoted to be the acting Superintendent of the Sunday school department. Through fasting, praying, and staying before the Lord the spirit of the Lord saw fit to anoint him to preach the gospel. He attended multiple Seminaries, and schools such as Howard University (School of Divinity), George Washington University, Morris Brown College in Atlanta Georgia, American Bible Society, and the Mrs. Green School of Music.

While sitting in a church service at the Tri Stone Fire Baptized Holiness Church, God spoke to Bishop Ford and told him to "Go to 1301 H. Street N.E. and build me a church." It was the voice of the Lord on that day that manifested itself into the great, spiritual powerhouse we know today as the St. John Church of God.

The St. John Church of God held its first service on December 5, 1971 in the former Cannon Shoe store building. Bishop Ford was humble to God's directive to build a church. Who knew this storefront building was leased for only $325 a month, would eventually turn into what it is today. By 1973 the Lord made provisions for Bishop Ford to purchase the building with a twelve-year mortgage. The church was paid off in nine years. In addition to paying the church off, Bishop Ford was able to purchase the restaurant next door to the church.

The storefront Church was a place where people came to get delivered and saved from their sins. The St. John Church of God was officially operating under the power of the Lord through the stern and powerful leadership of this great Bishop, who was a no-nonsense Bishop.

The prophecy came forth, "Now is the Time to Build." On February 2, 1980 the St. John Church temporarily relocated to the basement of the Douglas Memorial Church located at 11th and H. Street NE, so work could begin on building a new church. During this time the church's membership decreased to only 18 members. This was not a setback instead it was a part of God's bigger plan.

In March the same year, construction began on a brand-new sanctuary. The Storefront building and the adjoining restaurant building were razed and the foundation was set. Just as the contractors were ready to begin building, the church was more than ten-thousand dollars short on the fees they needed to begin.

Many banks in the area were no longer granting loans due to a freeze on funds and the money was not there. Bishop Ford was not discouraged. He continued to encourage the members to keep their focus on God during that time of uncertainty. He knew God would make the way. He also knew the voice of the Lord had spoken and God was going to perform that which He had spoken.

Despite the temporary financial situation, Bishop Ford single handedly continues to work himself every day, except Sunday. In August, 1980, God allowed Bishop Ford to secure a loan from the Capital City Federal Savings and Loan Association, to continue the work on the church. This allowed the contractors to return to the church the next day with 16 bricks masons and the wall went up in one day.

Bishop Ford and the members of the St. John Church of God moved into their brand-new church on December 5, 1980, just as Bishop said. Within four years of moving into the new building the mortgage was paid in full to Capitol City Federal Savings and Loan Association. God also allowed the church to purchase two houses around the corner on 13th Street.

People were amazed at how the Lord moved for St. John Church of God. The church was built on faith. God spoke the word and he continued to make the way. Bishop Ford was truly a great leader and a great man of God; a "package deal" with so many talents. If there had not been a Jesse Ford, Jr., there would not be a St. John Church of God.

Although Bishop Ford had many roles in the church, he was also grooming a young up and coming female minister, Sallie Bruce. This was rare because during this era in churches, and historically females were not chosen to be taught in these particular arenas. However, Bishop Ford was a progressive man of God, and did as the Lord told him he also understood that the Word could come from any vessel as long as this vessel presented themselves Holy and sanctified.

Chapter Two

The Legacy of Sallie A. Bruce

The connection between Bishop Ford, and Minister Bruce was certainly a strong one. Sallie Bruce was one of the first members of the St. John Church of God, and had the opportunity to preach her initial sermon there in 1973. Minister Bruce was a very reliable worker for the church, she worked in many positions including secretary, treasurer, Sunday school teacher, van driver, kitchen cook, and the fundraiser coordinator. She put in many years of dedication and hard work.

Bishop Ford had planned to ordain and promote her in July of 1985 during the Sunday School Convention as Reverend Bruce. He had even gone on record saying that if anything ever happened to him, he wanted them to get with Minister Bruce and carry on the work he accomplished in the church.

Bishop Ford died at the young age of 46 on June 3, 1985 and his Home Going service was held on June 8, 1985. Upon his sudden death this left the St. John Church of God without a pastor. Although he had gone on record saying that if anything ever happened to him, he wanted his congregation to follow Minister Bruce, it didn't stop other preachers from coming in and saying that St. John Church of God should continue with a male pastor. These preachers even went so far as to have phone calls that came through the St. John's phone lines be transferred to their personal phones in order to try and become the next pastor of the church.

Minister Bruce called to see if my sister Mary Walker, and myself would be able to nurse for the Home Going services for Bishop Ford. It was custom in the "old church" to get permission from our Pastor before we did something at another church. So, we had asked my Pastor, Bishop Robert Simpson Jr. if it would be okay for us to do this, and he graciously consented to it.

Bishop Harold Benjamin who was an old friend of the late Bishop Ford, and Bishop Benjamin preached his home going services. He then assisted Minister Bruce as she settled into her new position as the leader of the St. John Church of God. Bishop Benjamin organized a tribunal of church Elders which included the following men and women of God: Elder George Davis, Bishop John I. Little, and Mother Emma Young. They met and decided that Minister Bruce would be officially installed on the fourth Sunday in September of 1985 to become the pastor of the St. John Church of God.

Mother Young then took Minister Bruce downtown Washington D.C. to the courthouse to obtain a state license. So as Minister Bruce carried out the Sunday school convention in that year, and as planned she was officially installed as the pastor of the St. John Church of God Incorporated on the fourth Sunday in September of 1985. It was an amazing service, and Mary and I were once again called upon to nurse for the service.

Many in other churches came to support the service of the installation of Pastor Bruce as she was ordained and installed. And as an installation gift she was presented with a 1985 canary yellow Cadillac, and she was so appreciative with this first gift of her being a pastor. She did prove to be an extremely hard worker and dedicated pastor; she always went above and beyond to ensure her ministry ran smoothly.

Distraction came from the family of the late Bishop Ford; they decided they wanted money for the church as well as a house around the corner that the church had purchased. Both were still in Bishop Ford's name; due to his untimely death he hadn't had the chance to legally put both properties in the church's name. Therefore, the family was awarded the property where the home was, and to add further insult to injury the family further sued the church for $100,000.00, but Pastor Bruce continued to move forward in spite of everything.

I recall one day in October Pastor Bruce received a notice from the youth leader Evangelist Velma Nelson that she would be leaving, as the Lord called her to be a pastor. Pastor Bruce knew she needed a temporary youth leader until the Lord sent her the right person. She called me and said she wanted to ask my pastor if I could become the temporary youth leader.

The position would require me to work with the youth on the third Sunday in each month (the third Sunday was designated as Youth Sunday's). My pastor agreed and in November of 1985 I started having rehearsals and youth meetings on Saturday afternoons. I recall the first song I taught called, "My Mind is made up, and I'm on My Way Up. Going to Hold My Head Up, Going on with the Lord."

As I worked with the youth department, I began to build a rapport and trust with them, and they began confiding in me about concerns they were having. These talks turned into "wrap sessions", where they were allowed to express themselves without judgment. In these sessions we talked about all things that concerned them, no subject was off limits and the Lord led me on how to relate to them and provide them with sound spiritual advice.

As I continued to work with the youth department on third Sunday's at the St. John Church of God, I was still a tithe paying member at my home church. My pastor was Bishop Robert Simpson, Jr. at the Washington Deliverance Evangelist Center. He graciously approved me to help out the ministry at St John's due to Pastor Bruce beginning her role as a full-time pastor. As I worked with the St. John's youth they began to grow, and my duties expanded.

I began coming on additional Sunday's as the ministry at St. John's grew, instead of only coming on third Sunday's. I began attending on first and second Sunday's while still remaining a member at Washington

Deliverance. Eventually the Lord began speaking to me about becoming a member at the St. John Church of God; I searched my heart because I wanted to ensure that this is what God wanted me to do. After much thought and prayer one Sunday I decided it was time for me to join the St. John family permanently.

Like all other Sundays Pastor Bruce offered people the opportunity to join the church if they didn't have a home church. I walked up with four other persons who wanted to join the church that day, Pastor Bruce welcomed them and gave them the right hand of fellowship. But when she got to me, she laughed and said to me, "I don't think so…" I was most embarrassed, but she said I couldn't join until she spoke to my pastor, Bishop Simpson.

After Pastor Bruce talked to my then pastor, Bishop Simpson he gave me his blessing to join the St. John Church of God. So when I left my home church I left the correct way, but not without the members saying things about me. Comments were being made such as I was crazy for leaving my home church that I had been a member since age eleven. I had grown up in the Washington Deliverance church; I was married there and had my children while being a member there. But my assignment there was over, and God had plans for me to work alongside Pastor Bruce to help build her ministry. And I had the blessing of my pastor.

Pastor Bruce's ministry began to grow in leaps and bounds, Pastor received her doctorate in the class of 1993 under the auspicious Christian Bible Institute; Dr. Donald Womack, President. In addition, the Lord elevated her to become Overseer. Services for her installation of consecration to the sacred office of Overseer took place on Saturday, July 16, 2005 at 11:00 a.m., and she also became the Overseer of multiple churches. She became known for her "no nonsense" style of leadership, and getting her congregation involved in her sermons as she took volunteers and utilized the entire stage for her amazing demonstrations.

Overseer Bruce became the covering for many churches such as, Pastor Albert Hanks of the Tree of Life Ministries in Waldorf Maryland, Pastor Eric Gordon of the New Hope Deliverance out of Columbus Ohio, Pastor Cassandra Lewis of the True Vine Church of God out of Columbus Ohio, Pastor Rebecca Carter of the Word of Faith and Hope Outreach Ministry out of Stone Mountain Georgia, Pastor Shirley Peacock of the Greater Faith Anointing Deliverance Ministries out of Decatur Georgia, Pastor Claritha Stewart of the Independent Church of God out of Washington, D.C. To these pastors and church bodies, and our friends who have proven faithful we thank you for the fellowship. We love you for loving us and taking time to celebrate with us over the years. I would be remiss if I do not give special thanks to our Ecclesiastical Tribunal Bishop Harold Benjamin, Elder George Davis, and Dr. John I. Little, and Mother Emma Young, who came to the aid of this church during some critical times.

She truly lived out what she preached and she continued to be a blessing as she brought the St. John Church of God into the 21st Century. I witnessed the true work of God in her life as she modeled what it meant to trust in God, depend on God, and stay in His perfect will regardless of what we face. I began to home in on my purpose as to why God brought me into this great ministry, I became Overseer Bruce's personal assistant and servant. St. John was on the move with plenty of action coming our way in the ministry.

As the years passed and the times changed, the ministry of St. John Church of God escalated to the next level in God, under the leadership of Overseer Bruce. She preached the Word of God on television through a weekly one hour "DNA" (Deliverance Now and Always) telecast. This telecast was very popular through DC cable and other state cable networks. Many souls were saved and several people joined the church as a result of the DNA telecast. She also began the long-standing Sunday morning radio broadcast on station 1120 WUST, and later on 1340 WYCB. God also allowed the St. John church to open the doors to the St. John Kiddie Kollege that expanded throughout the Washington, DC metropolitan area, with more than three locations at that time.

Overseer Bruce manifested her spiritual gifts with the evidence of laying on hands, wisdom, the gift of prophecy, discernment and the ability to speak things into existence through unwavering faith. Overseer Bruce was admired greatly by her church members, other churches within the community. She embedded the concept of holy and righteous living to her members and never compromised with worldly concepts just to build a membership.

She enforced rules of righteous living and she held her members to a high standard of holy expectations. Some of her mottos were, "All unrighteous is sin!" or "Get with the people who are going up." Or "With loving kindness have I drawn thee." Overseer Bruce did not play when it came to living right; she was known to have "the look." This was a look that captured her members, stopped them in their tracks and made them go before the Lord in forgiveness. She had such a connection with her congregation, that even a small look would make them evaluate their sins and get right.

Overseer Bruce was a teacher indeed. She taught her members and countless others to grow spiritually and morally. She led by example and preached well, some of her most infamous soul saving sermons were, "Watch your step." And "Who are you following?" Her sermons were always encouraging such as, "God is more than enough." And "Nobody knows the story behind my praise." Overseer Sallie Bruce's ministry grew over the years; she had the opportunity to preach in Georgia, North and South Carolina, New York, Arizona, California, Virginia, Delaware, Florida, Pennsylvania, Bahamas, and South America. As a result of her ministry souls were continuously saved, sanctified and filled with the Holy Ghost while others were healed, revived and reclaimed.

We also needed transportation for the church for the members who wanted to attend service but didn't have transportation. I remember Pastor Bruce calling one morning, and told me to pick her up, because we were going to purchase a bus for the church, and as usual I didn't question her. I did what I was told and picked her up and proceeded to the bus company. We met with the salesman and she told him what she wanted, and he in returned asked her, "Reverend how much money do you have to put down?

And she looked at me, and then turned back to the salesman and said, "I don't have any money…'. He then said, "Reverend how are you going to get this bus?" Pastor stated, "You are going to order it." We will do this and you will do that, and he did. Two months later we received a call that the bus was sent in from the manufacturer, and they asked her how she wanted the writing to appear on the bus, she said "Put the name of the church, the pastor's name and the telephone number to the church." And then she said, "See What the Lord has done."

And this is how God moved mightily at the St. John Church of God, always sending miraculous opportunities our way. And because our faith was great, we usually obtained what needed to help the ministry grow. Never forgetting that souls were our primary reason for existing. Overseer Bruce wanted all to know that God is for them, and if they desired God would change their lives forever. She welcomed all to come to the feast at the table of the Lord, and the businesses were a vehicle for the church to accomplish all things.

There were many new things and historical events happening at the St. John Church of God, Dr. Bruce was always up to something. For the first time in St. John's history she decided to install an assistant pastor, and no one had any idea she was led by God to choose her faithful servant Paulette Brockington. She told me the night before service, was just go along with whatever I say and or do in Sunday's service. Servant Brockington had no idea what was about to happen or take place, and so at Sunday's service Dr. Bruce made the grand announcement that for the first time in history at St. Johns' church she installed an assistant pastor.

In 2010 Overseer Bruce celebrated 25 years in her silver Pastoral anniversary. It was a milestone in the history of the St. John's church and it was a moment to remember. It was an extravaganza to be reckoned with and people came from near and far to celebrate with her. Less than one year later she suffered a stroke, but God kept her mind and continued to work through her. Although Overseer Bruce was physically confined to a wheelchair, she preached God's Word in season and out of season. She was a living example of the faith and hope she preached about. Overseer Bruce continued to teach and preach God's Word and she constantly sought the Lord for everything.

God spoke to Overseer Bruce concerning the St. John Church of God located on H Street. In 2013, Overseer Bruce announced "After carrying out Bishop Ford's vision for twenty-eight years, it is now time for me to carry out my own vision and legacy. We are building a new church." God told Overseer Bruce to build a new church. She was so excited about this new church as she designed it exactly how God gave it to her. She worked with the contractors while drawing up the plans. She made change after change until it was exactly what she wanted. Overseer Bruce urged every member in the church to get themselves together. She stated, "We are not taking any mess into this new church." She made new appointments within the church auxiliaries and she met with the president of each committee. She put people in place and she set the house in order.

On December 26, 2013 Overseer Bruce was called home to Glory to be with the Lord. Her legacy will forever live through her members. Her many memories of righteous living will forever reside in the hearts of everyone, who had the pleasure of knowing her. Without Overseer Sallie Bruce's vision and ministry there would be no St. John Church of God, she carried out the Lord's work until her last days. Her last sermon was called, "Breathe on me and let me live." Those were the final set of instructions she gave to the church. God breathed on Overseer Bruce and her legacy will continue to live through the St. John Church of God. And her vision will be fulfilled, and her plans will be carried out.

Chapter Three

The Servant Paulette Brockington Becomes the Leader

The Mantle has Been Passed Down

Just as God saw fit for Overseer Bruce to step into position as pastor after Bishop Ford went home to be with Lord, God blessed St. John Church of God once again. This time there was no pastoral "search committee", resumes were not being accepted, and there was no need for an interim pastoral appointee. God had the right person already in the midst. God had a woman who was ready and anointed to carry out this ministry. And that was Assistant Pastor Paulette Brockington; she humbly stepped into position as pastor of the St. John Church of God on December 26, 2013, and she was officially installed on March 29, 2014.

Now officially being the pastor of the St. John Church of God. During this time, she represented the will of God in every aspect of her ministry. She's demonstrated Holy living and an unyielding work of excellence to build the house of God. Some of her most encouraging sermons this past year have been, "I'm Anointed for this", "Stabilize, stay focused and don't get crazy on me now", "Help wanted", and "It's time for a reality check." These sermons have strengthened the congregation and taught them to dig deep inside for a change.

Her ministry is truly a ministry of love, dedication and support. It offers the members of St. John a guide to living right. She maintains a close relationship with her members. She urges them to come directly to her if they don't understand something or if there is anything they need to know. She promotes working in the church and supports anyone willing to work. She, unlike a lot of pastors, will make the time for her members. You don't have to go through an entire staff to make an appointment; she's right there. You can also depend on her for honesty and direct responses.

During this short time as pastor of the St. John Church of God, she has secured many ways to ensure a solid foundation for the new sanctuary of the St. John Church of God. It is her vision to have a church where ministry can be the focus, regardless of what comes across the offering table. She's been blessed with a keen sense of business skills. Her dedication to the ministry and God serves as an example that many set out to follow. Most importantly the new vision she has as a great leader has impacted many. The congregation has increased in paying tithes, souls have grown closer to the Lord and the members are learning how to overcome the obstacles of life, while remaining faithful to God.

This year alone, she has taken the DC metropolitan area by storm. In December, of 2014 she opened the St. John kitchen, a soul food carry out that was second to none in Southeast Washington DC. She was also inducted into the Women's Business Alliance, as well as honored by WYCB radio station, as one of the top pastors in the DC area. These accomplishments are a prime example of the favor of God has on her life. Her hard work and commitment haven't gone unnoticed. Although there have been a lot of changes and things thrown at her this past year, she continues to soar closer to the vision that God gave her. She continues to stand in the midst of uncertainty and adversity as she seamlessly transitions into her new role as pastor. This first pastoral year was a success and she was excited for what lies ahead for herself and the St. John Church of God.

Her favorite scripture Matthew 6:33 But seek ye first the kingdom of God, and his righteousness; and all these things shall be added unto you. It is this scripture that has served as the guiding light to her life and her ministry. She firmly believes that you must serve God wholeheartedly and dedicate your life to giving God the glory. When we put our time and energy into seeking God, He will truly make provision for the things we need while on earth. There is nothing God can't do.

Pastor Paulette Brockington came from humble beginnings, she is the youngest of five children, and she was born to the late James and Margaret Powell. She is a native of Washington DC, she was raised in the North East section on the ridge of Capitol Hill. She was educated in the DC public school system attending Walker Jones Elementary, Shaw Junior High and graduating from Cardozo High School. Upon graduation, she attended the DC Business Institute. Subsequently other interests pointed her into the health field where she was trained in dialysis at the children's hospital, and a phlebotomist. She worked at several hospitals during the subsequent years.

She began her Christian experience at the Greater Washington Deliverance Temple. She was saved, educated and guided under the leadership of Pastor Robert Simpson, Jr. and Evangelist Ida M. Simpson. In 1963 she married the love of her life, Roosevelt Brockington, Sr. this union resulted in the birth of four children: Rosalind, Regina, Roosevelt, Jr., and Robert Brockington. In 1985, with her administrative skills, she was dispatched on loan to assist Pastor Sallie A. Bruce, who was newly installed, to assist with the youth department.

In 1988 she joined the ministry full time; her ministry with St. John has afforded her the opportunity to work in many positions. Such as secretary, treasurer, promoter, fundraiser, event planner, director and administrator of the St. John Kiddie Kollege. She also attended the Christian Bible Institute, Bloomfield Township New Jersey. Subsequently, in an effort to further develop her skills, she obtained a Bachelor of Science degree in early childhood education from Bowie University in 2009. In addition, she is also the best radio announcer on this side of heaven, and her introductions are second to none. She's traveled extensively in and out of the United States.

As a bible schoolteacher, she believes in open forums and providing people the opportunity to take God's Word and learn of it, as well as apply it directly to their situation. As a Sunday school teacher, she always encourages her class to make real life decisions as it pertains to the Word of God. She is known to infuse God's Word into daily living and she never sugar coats anything. She breaks down the Word of God in a way that even a small child can understand it. Her sermons are life changing, thought provoking and often leave one examining themselves.

Her ministry is truly a ministry of love, dedication and support. It offers the members of St. John a guide to living right. She maintains a close relationship with my members. She urges them to come directly to her if they don't understand something or if there is anything they need to know. She promotes working in the church and supports anyone willing to work. She, unlike a lot of pastors, will make the time for her members. You don't have to go through an entire staff to make an appointment; she's right there. You can also depend on her for honesty and direct responses.

During this short time as pastor of the St. John Church of God, she has secured many ways to ensure a solid foundation for the new sanctuary of the St. John Church of God. It is her vision to have a church where ministry can be the focus, regardless of what comes across the offering table. She's been blessed with a keen sense of business skills. Her dedication to the ministry and God serves as an example that many set out to follow. Most importantly the new vision she has as a great leader has impacted many. The congregation has increased in paying tithes, souls have grown closer to the Lord and the members are learning how to overcome the obstacles of life, while remaining faithful to God.

Chapter Four
When the Servant Leader Bleeds

A Time of Reflection?

As I reflect on my journey from a servant to a leader, in hindsight I faced many challenges and had to overcome them. There were many times my spirit was bleeding out but I could not stop, I had to keep moving forward in God's faith. If someone would've told me that my journey would've been as big a challenge as it was I might've not willfully went on the journey. But this was my calling, and I heeded the calling even though it cost me along the way. My dearest son was murdered, I eventually lost my beloved Pastor, and through all of this I had become leader. So what happens when the servant leader bleeds?

As I reflect upon my journey, I'm reminded of the song that says, I don't believe He brought me this far to leave me. Let's take a look back at my amazing journey. During these busy times with the church annual events, and being assistant pastor my son was tragically murdered while he was at work. In most circumstances everything should've paused, but somehow, I found the strength to continue on. While there was nothing more important than the loss of my son who was my husband's name sake, somehow, I kept on going in supporting the ministry.

My heart was bleeding for the loss of my child, and I along with my family planned his home going services, and Dr. Bruce was scheduled to preach his eulogy, however tragedy struck again. Dr. Bruce suffered a stroke. I urged her to go to the hospital to get herself checked out but she insisted she was fine so we continued, but because of the stroke she wasn't able to preach my son's eulogy. Now in hindsight this should've been the one time I disobeyed my great leader, and with hindsight being 2020 no one knew that the stroke would forever change the dynamic of our lives and the ministry. But God!

There was a lot going on, my son's home going service, and my leader was going through with her health issues. Directly after my son's services were complete, I went straight to the hospital to see Dr. Bruce. These were truly times of uncertainty, and I was dealing with so much on my plate but I stayed at the hospital with my leader only leaving to go home and shower, or to manage the daycare business. My heart and my mind were so full, again I should've paused but life, events, and business were demanding my attention. I had to keep going.

Now I am dealing with two tragedies, the death of my son and my leader has suffered a stroke, and I must also keep the ministry afloat. While most of our members were faithful and committed uncertainty can bring about unrest among the flock. It was a great challenge for me to juggle the added responsibilities of continuing on as the assistant pastor, as Dr. Bruce's future weighed in the balance. We were uncertain if she would make a full recovery or if the stroke would have a permanent effect on her, so we waited with anticipation to see how she would recover from the stroke.

After Dr. Bruce stayed in the hospital for a while, she was released to go to rehabilitation. And like a true servant leader I followed her to the rehabilitation establishment, and also stayed with her there. When you are a true servant you follow your leader in all places of their lives. When I say I am "servant" I mean that in action and deed not just a title or a moniker. My servitude was likened unto the servants in the bible, if their leader/master went up so the servant. If the leader/master went down so did the servant, through the good the bad, and the ugly the servant was by their leader/master's side. And I served Dr. Bruce well.

She and I fought many battles together, tore down strongholds, when the enemy came one way, we sent him packing seven different ways. Being on the battlefield wasn't anything new to her and I, we operated fully by our faith in God. And it was God that always gave the victory. So here we are again fighting another battle, but this battle is personal. When the enemy attacked the ministry, I was ready for it and understood how to fight back, but this battle hit home and I found myself discombobulated. Just as if in the natural you were in a physical fight, and your opponent sucker punches you while you're not looking.

The same is in the spirit, I've been spiritually suckered punched, but I was taught well when engaging in warfare. Sometimes a good fighter has to step back, regroup themselves, re-strategize and get back in the heat of the battle. It would be safe to say that the enemy picked a fight with the wrong duo, what happened to my leader was as if God was boasting about her commitment to Him. Just as in the bible he asked Satan hast thou considered my servant Job? Dr. Bruce was considered by God, and I being her servant was also considered, and in the ministry world as a leader or a servant you will be tested, tried, and proved.

Although Dr. Bruce suffered the stroke, she was always a resilient woman, and she continued to pastor, and preach for years. Although she was refined to a wheelchair, there were many occasions she willed herself to stand up without assistance from anyone as the anointing fell heavy upon her as she bought the word forth. Dr. Bruce was still fully operating the church she kept her speaking engagements; she traveled to spread the word of God. Those were truly some amazing moments. There were many occasions as our church associates would say I was going to be the pastor of the church, but I let them know immediately that Dr. Bruce would be the pastor of St. John Church of God until she closes her eyes permanently.

As my 50th year wedding anniversary approached, Dr. Bruce insisted that my husband and I renew our vows, and she planned the whole event. So I asked her to be my maid of honor, and as the wedding ceremony started. Dr. Bruce surprised everyone again with her resiliency and in Dr. Bruce style and to defy her illness she surprised everyone by walking down the aisle as the Maid of Honor. Needless to say there wasn't a dry eye in the house, and everyone said she stole the show. It was times like this that I know she had great faith and a strong-willed spirit in spite of her disability. She also knew we needed a welcomed distraction from all we had just been through, so out of tragedy she showed us how to continue to celebrate with each other.

Dr. Bruce wasn't only my leader over the years we became very close friends, as the bible says a friend will stick closer than a brother. The person that maliciously murdered my son had been arraigned in court, it was exceedingly difficult for me to sit in the court and look at my son's murderer. There were many times I sat outside of the courtroom during these proceedings. But Dr. Bruce was there every day we had to go to court, and she sat in for me along with my husband and other family members. She was a true friend, and she said she wanted to look at this person who took my son from me; I appreciated her so much for her friendship.

Chapter Five
The Bonus Chapter

"The Announcer Speaks!"

{Pastor Paulette Brockington was interviewed by the Publisher of this book, Sean Cort, continue reading about her ideas or thoughts about her journey from servant to leader.}

A t the time of the writing of this book our nation is in utter tumult. It appears that the change that is required is not driven by the leadership of one man or women but the passion that permeates an entire generation of youth of all nations and cultures. This passion is succeeding in swifter change that resonates on the level of our nation's conscience rather than its legislation.

On the other hand, resilience, commitment and sacrifice is what keeps the dialogue of and for change churning. Social scientists have concluded that because baby boomers and generation Xers as parents have withheld the examples of sacrifice, resilience and commitment from the current millennial and generation Z demographic in an attempt to be better providers.

This term is coined in the phrase, "helicopter parents" due to our tendency to hover over our children in a proverbial manner that keeps the sun from burning their skin or scorching their spirit. Thus we have a passionate cause without leadership. To address this chasm of what servant leadership looks like today as compared to the generation of Rev. Brockington, we will summon creative license and conclude the balance of this autobiography as a Q & A format to appeal to the next generation of torch bearers. – Sean Cort

Q. Why is it important to you to write a book about years serving someone in the ministry?

It is important to me to write this book about my servitude and leadership, because I wanted to help someone, and they can perhaps use my experience and apply it to their own journey. Serving or leading isn't an easy job, you won't be winning any popularity contests because as a servant or leader you will have to make hard decisions that most times won't be pleasing to those who choose to follow you. In I Peter 5:2, (CEB) to paraphrase this scripture it says that persons who watch over God's flock we don't do it to because we have to but we answered the call of God to protect and keep his people. So, it's not about fame or notoriety because as a leader or servant this role in the church is very challenging and can be difficult. We as servants/leaders must learn to juggle many balls or wear many hats to be an effective servant or leader.

The same challenges that leaders and Christians faced back in the bible days are basically the same challenges servant/leaders face today. In I Corinthians 9:19-23, the Apostle Paul said although he was a free man, he chose to make himself a slave to all people to win as many souls for Christ as possible. To the Jew he became as a Jew, to those under the law, he became like one under the law, although he wasn't under the law. To those not under the law, he became like those not under the law, (but always acting under the law of God). To those who are weak, he too became weak, he became all things to all people as to win souls for Christ. He did these things for the sake of the gospel that he might save some. The

Apostle Paul wanted to identify and appeal to all people, in other words his leadership had to be fluid he had to understand the needs of the people who came from different backgrounds, cultures, and lifestyles. He wasn't subscribing that we should break the law by being unlawful, but he had to understand and meet the needs of the persons he was serving. It is the same for servants/leaders in the 21st century, we must be all things to all people in order to understand how to meet their needs and lead them. As a servant/leader we must be fluid, because people in today's culture are faced with many different types of challenges. People's lives are very complex and intertwined in those complexities are a barrage of issues we all have to deal with and figure out how to overcome them successfully.

My role as a servant I had to serve mainly one person who was my pastor, but she was serving many persons so her leadership responsibilities at times flowed into my duties as her servant. Being her servant for those few decades is where I learned to perfect my role as servant and years later this experience would help me transition into a successful leader. Essentially you have one person watching over the souls of many persons, and once I became a leader there were times I had to dig deep in God to get the "know how" to lead His people and this is not always easy to do. And this is why I wanted to write this book, I want young and upcoming leaders to know that with hard work, dedication, and keeping God the center of your journey it is possible to succeed and do miraculous things in God.

Whatever stage you are in your leadership, whether you've been leading for years or just beginning your journey my story will be relevant to you as a leader or servant. Although I was saves at the age of 14, I didn't start my servant/leader journey until I was age 39. Now my journey began a little later in my life, but all servant/leaders will be faced with the same challenges, this journey is not about age or status God will call whom He will, and whom will be willing to obey His calling to serve or lead. Is God calling you? And will you answer His call?

Are you willing to go through the fire and be tried? Whatever your answers are to these questions just know you won't be popular, and you won't get famous, but what you will have is a lot of late nights laying before God seeking Him for the next steps. You'll be in your prayer closet regularly asking God for His direction on how to lead His people, and to give you the strength to endure hardness as good soldier. Because the same people who love you, or hail you, they will be the same people that will nail you the cross just as they did our Savior. I encourage you to only be a servant or leader if you're called by God.

Q. At what point did you realize you're a Servant Leader? Was there a process in becoming a Servant Leader or was natural for you?

I was most comfortable in my role as a servant, I never wanted to lead. I was satisfied with being a servant, but I heard someone say if you want to hear God laugh tell Him your plans. He certainly had other plans for me, however I had come to perfect my servant role. It was something I enjoyed doing, I didn't have to be out in front but was happy serving my pastor and making sure she had all she needed to lead the people of God. Unbeknownst to me through her tutelage and being around her so much I was being groomed and sharpened to be what God would eventually have me to be which was the next leader of the St. John Church of God.

Becoming a leader is somewhat more of a complex process, leaders are not born, but made. My pastor was a person who did all things in excellence and being around her and seeing her dedication to God, the people she served, and the church couldn't help but have a profound effect on me. This effect was so gradual that at first I hadn't noticed just how much I had learned from her, but I found myself growing and expanding as I was serving her. I guess you can say I was oblivious to deep affect her examples of a leader had taken on myself. But as she and I continued to work closely side by side what was already inside of me, and the way our spirits agreed and our journey's being parallel now in hindsight I can see how God was moving in my life to have me transition from a servant to a leader.

And when you think about it a servant and leader roles share many similarities, you have to be available to the person(s) you're serving or leading 24/7. Either role isn't a job that has set hours, you don't set the hours the hours set you. Either role means you have to have a close and personal relationship with God, you must live close to Him, and be a studier and doer of His word. This is the only way you can be effective in either role. In our naivety we look at a pastor's role and think this is the life or part we want to be in. And because over the years the "new Age" church have sensationalized the role of leader or pastor as being a celebrity/famous. Some leaders are infatuated with this title, or getting the attention that this role can carry because instead of God getting the glory, they are getting the glory.

I'm reminded of a passage of scripture in Matthews 20:20, where the mother of James and John asked Jesus for a favor. She asked Jesus to allow her sons to sit on either side of Him in the Kingdom. The bible doesn't make us aware of the mother's intention but what a heavy request to ask Jesus and without giving Him good cause why her sons should sit on the right and left side of God in His Kingdom. One's intention and purpose must be pure as to why you want to be a servant or leader, you shouldn't do it for fame or notoriety. Jesus went on to ask the mother is her sons ready to take part in the bitter cup He knew He was going to have to endure, and they answered too quickly, yes. Jesus informed them that they didn't know what they were asking for, but He did let them know they would be drinking from the cup of bitterness. But whomever sits on either side of Him will be up to His Father in heaven.

I agree with Jesus's answer to the mother and her sons that they had no idea what they were asking for. This role as a pastor on the outside can look extremely attractive, it appears that you get a lot of attention and recognition. But anyone who quickly runs into this role makes me question their intentions, the pressure of this kind of duty can weigh heavily on your spirit. A pastor is responsible for the health and well-being of His children and as leaders we have to be very careful how we entreat God's special gifts. One wouldn't want to find themselves on the wrong side of God's mercy, which is His wrath for caring improperly for His children. When I see folk running to sign up to be a pastor it concerns me because I know that these are the ones who went, and not have been sent. Truly no one readily runs into this role as a leader because if you've witnessed true leadership that is dedicated to God, you know this road isn't easy. Because either you'll know or will learn there will be many sleepless nights, the days will not be your own, but they will belong to the flock you're leading.

Your immediate family and loved ones will suffer because there will be many days and nights that you'll have to sacrifice spending time with them because the call to duty is upon you. And I hope your family is one that is supportive of your calling, if not this makes the calling even more challenging because often times, they're going through the same things you are as a leader. This role will bleed into every part of your life, and it will take over your life so you must be decisive that God called you specifically for this role, otherwise it will take its' toll on you and all those that are affected by what you do. Now if you're called it may have the same affect but because God honors family you may not go unscathed, but your family will remain intact. My advice to you is be sure you're the one who was sent, and not the one who went.

Q. Was there a process in becoming a Servant Leader or was natural for you?

There was certainly a definitive process in me becoming a servant leader, I just wasn't privy to God's plan in the beginning of my journey. And as I said earlier in my story, the journey getting to the destination wasn't linear. God's plans for our lives is so amazing and grand that He can't show us the full plan all at once I don't think our human minds could take it. But he spoons feeds us the plan as we mature spiritually and as our faith grows stronger. Take for example I'm a mother, and when my children were little babies you feed them, test them, and try them in the stages of their years. I was a babe in Christ so the Lord had lots to teach me and show me before I could go to the next steps of this process.

As my children grew their lessons in life grew, after crawling for so long they automatically started pulling up on the coffee tables to stand after discovering that their little legs could do more than scoot around on the floor. And me as their mother would encourage them that they could do it, and that's how the journey with God is, He helps us along the way encouraging us building our faith testing us to believe bigger, and stronger. Just like a mother when my children began to walk, and as they became more confident the walking turned into running, and when they fell down and cried I was there to pick them up and encourage them that they were okay. I picked them up and they took off again, and so this becomes a process them testing out new things that they discovered their bodies could do, and when they fell down, as a mother I was there to pick them up and encourage them that they could do it.

This is similar to the process that God had me go through, crawling, before I could walk, walking before I could run, and then finally when I was allowed or able to run in the spirit God had to teach me to pace myself. True leaders are not born but made; my late pastor was an excellent mentor she was patient with me. Although her lessons were not always pleasant to learn however when you're sharpening iron this process can be unpleasant and uncomfortable but, in the end, according to II Timothy 2:3 you're made to endure hardness as a good soldier. I can say from experience that this walk of life isn't for everybody, because we're going to have to mimic some of the same challenges that Jesus went through when he walked the earth. You will suffer in this life, further in this same chapter of II Timothy 2 to paraphrase verses 11 – 13 if we die in God we will live, if we endure or suffer with Him we will reign with Him. If we deny Him; He'll deny us but if we're unfaithful to Him. He will remain faithful because the scripture says He can't be anything other than what He is, faithful to us. My servant leader journey wasn't an organic or natural process it was a spiritual and awakening process. I had to be made as a servant leader and made into a leader.

Q. Please list your process to moving from leader to servant leader, what are the earmarks of a servant compared to a servant leader.

My journey from a servant to a leader has many of the same characteristics before you lead one must be able to follow. Effective leadership means that I was able to follow and execute instructions as a servant perfectly. Although I wasn't always perfect, I had the desire to follow my late pastor and help her be a success and in doing so I was perfecting my own abilities as a leader. Under my late pastor's tutelage, I learned humility, I learned to listen because listening is essential. I learned to be obedient, and this is an area where a lot of would be great leaders fell because they feel that obeying another human being is subservient. My late pastor truly had the power of God in and on her life, and as a servant I saw this so accepting her requests as her servant wasn't hard for me to do. One I believed in her leadership abilities, and a lot of her beliefs were the same as my own, two our journeys in life ran parallel there were a lot of similarities in how God was moving in our lives, and third this is what God had called me to do, and being obedient first to God made it easy to understand why I was on this servant leader journey.

As a servant one has to want to help in whatever capacity they can, a servant has to love those that they are serving and wants to genuinely see them do well. And is willing to help them accomplish said goals to help them reach their accomplishments. A servant has to have a discerning spirit to think ahead, and troubleshoot any would be issues, problems, or roadblocks that might impede the progress of those that they serve. The servant is always watchful, always looking without to be ahead of any problems or issues that could arise, a good servant is always a step ahead. If a problem or issue does arise, a good servant has the ability to think quickly on their feet and find an effective solution to the problem or issues. A good servant is always thinking ahead and always preparing always being ready for whatever comes their way and is willing to make sure the person (s) they serve has everything they need without being told. A great servant will study those they serve, learn their leaders' habits, pays attention to the details. In doing so a servant could make their leaders processes look like seamless transactions. What I said about a servant is exactly what a great leader would do, the characteristics are very similar.

Q. What is the key premise in being a Godly and successful leader?

Love is the premise for being a Godly leader and successful leader. You must love God first and then love those that you're serving. You truly have to have a spirit to want to help people and see them grow in their full potential in God. The Gospel is the good news of God, and when you accept the call to spread the gospel all others things become secondary. It also doesn't hurt to take a course that will help you be a successful leader, I often wonder why as a people we will go to school to learn trades, get degrees, or just take an enjoyable pottery class. But somehow, we won't take a course on effective leadership, as I said before leaders are not born but made. First you should wait to see if this is a calling on your life to lead or serve because unless it is down in your bones to do either you might find it difficult to walk this path. Lastly and most importantly you have to be filled with the precious gift of the Holy Ghost and live a saved and sanctified life free and separate from sin.

Your followers are looking for an example, they look at their leader not always having to be perfect, but as a leader you must have something to offer them. You're leading God's people to live a life also free and separate from sin, as a leader you must give them something to look forward to in Christ. Followers look to their leaders to provide them with practical and godly principles on how to manage everyday living through the Word of God. God's words inspire the leader and in return the leader shares what God has given them; however, it works both ways. A leader is only as strong as the followers, if the followers are not thriving, then that means that there's a break down in the effectiveness of the leader. But if the leader is ensuring to stay and lay before God seeking Him on what and how to lead His people it is guaranteed success with the followers and the leader. A great leader is always seeking God, constantly in prayer, and prayer means that they are communicating with God, soon your gift in God will make room for you and you will have something to share with God's people.

Q. (A) Please describe yourself in third person/what are your Strengths:

If I was to describe myself in third person, I would say that Paulette Brockington is first a woman who loves her husband; the love of her life Roosevelt Brockington, Sr. before him there was none and after him there will be no more. She is a mother of four children, a grandmother of eight children, and a great grandmother of five children. Paulette Brockington is a pastor/servant of the St. John Church of God, she's a bible guru, and she's a mentor to young women. She's an example of a godly woman, always evolving and learning to please God, she's a force to reckon with, a woman of great faith. Lastly Paulette Brockington is an overcomer, according to I John 5:4, it says whatsoever is born of God over cometh the world and this is the victory that over cometh the world, even our faith.

B. What are personal obstacles God had to work through in you?

This is a very good question because often time's leaders are afraid to show their areas of opportunity for growth or development. And I am ever evolving and changing to remain relevant as a leader in a very competitive culture. I feel it's important to be transparent and open to let your followers know that you have struggles, and difficulties as everyone does. My answer to this question may come as surprise to those who've only known me to respect and love my leaders. But the area of opportunity that God wanted me to perfect was having respect for leadership, how to entreat leadership, and have respect for the house of God. Now before you all string me up, for admitting my areas of growth is the very thing that God had as my journey let me expound. You see only God knows the full plan for ones' life, and what journey He will call you for. As I said earlier God cannot show us the full picture all at once because most of us would take off running in the other direction. God knew that I was one day going to be a leader and have a house of God where we the people of God would come together to worship.

So, yes God had to teach me how to respect leaders, entreat them and respect the house of God, that these things are precious gifts and should be given the reverence that He intended for them to have. I did have a lot of problems with understanding the level of respect I needed to have in order to be pleasing to God so there was some work for me to do in this area of my life. In the book of I Corinthian 12:31, it says for me to covet earnestly the best gifts and yet shew I unto you a more excellent way. As a servant and leader, God had to show me a more excellent way, and now I understand and know how to protect Gods' sacred place, His house is a place where His spirit dwells and one must come in with the right spirit as to not to upset or disturb His movement. So if I see God's house not being reverenced or if I see a leader not being respected it is my job to cry aloud and spare not, to lift my voice up like a trumpet and show the people their transgressions according to Isaiah 58:1.

A leader must be able to stand on God's Word and speak with a Holy boldness what He says for me to say. This can be uncomfortable at times because who wants to hurt people's feelings or delve out hard lessons. But I must obey God's Words just the same as if I were giving out the blessings of God, along with blessings comes corrections and instructions. Proverbs 4:13 says take fast hold of instruction; let not her go: keep her; for she is thy life. But I have to be the first partaker according to II Timothy 2:6. Any corrections or lessons that had to be learned had to come to me first to teach me so that I can be an effective leader. It's mighty hard to be a leader who has no experience in what they are teaching. God has to take me through the courses and changes to make me what He wanted me to be, and although I felt I always had deep respect for leaders and the house of God, I had to be taught a deeper respect and grow a deeper love for the leaders and His house.

C. What's struggles and strength do you see in younger Servant leaders and their generation.

First let me talk about the struggles or opportunities I see in today's younger servant/leaders. I feel they lack patience, partly it's not their fault; millennials/Centennials are born into the point and click era. So they are not necessarily built to wait for things in life to mature due to technology always has them living in the fast lane, and there's little or no opportunity for them to stop and smell the roses. Another disadvantage and great

struggle I see in today's young servant/leaders is that they don't study historical data on how something or things came to be. I feel they are quick to replace the old with the new or technology so much so until they could be missing out on very valuable information because they see old instead of gold. They must understand that history, is the very foundation they are building their brand-new technology on, its' history's back that is holding up the strong foundation. While the Millennials/Centennials is our future servant/leaders they need to understand the history or origin of how the foundation was made for them to build upon.

The strengths of the servant/leader is definitely built in technology, and they are innovative they can take processes and streamline them to be more efficient and work more effectively. I feel we need a balance of both the old and new to make great future servant/leaders, we need each other to show each other the importance of each generation how we all can make a positive impact in our churches, communities, states, and ultimately the country. I say they need the older generation and the older generation need the younger generation. While I'm willing to embrace the new age processes and innovations some things just don't change. If they want to know God deeply and learn His ways that has to be done the old-fashioned way through much fasting and prayer per the book of Matthews chapter 17, verse 21. Seeking and laying before God, and getting deep in His Word, this process cannot be altered to fit into technology you must go down on your face before God like the old saints did there is no technology "fix" that can gain God accept you be born again.

Q. How does being a servant leader translate to everyday life society?

I live a life that honors God, and in this life, you have to be a people person because your life really isn't you own anymore. I have to stay prayed up and be vigilant because God wants us to be instant in season and out of season per the scripture in II Timothy 4:2, I stay ready as to not having to get ready. Most importantly you have to be a kind person a leader has to be friendly to all people per adventure we can draw some to Christ; it says in Jeremiah 31:3, with loving kindness have I drawn thee. It's important for leaders to be relatable, I have to appeal to all walks of life all must see the God in me for it is Him that draws the people to me. A great leader has the ability to take God's Word and apply it to everyday life, and make the Word relatable to life. The bible is the answer to all of our problems in Ecclesiastes 1:9, it says and there is no new thing under the sun.

Everything we need we can find in the Word of God, but it's my job to help you find your connection through God's Word, and then show you how to apply it to your everyday life.

Q. Was there an ever a time when you didn't want the mantle of being servant leader and, if so, when and why?

Yes, there's been so many times, when I see people running to fill in a pastor's position or a role of a servant/leader I don't trust the authenticity of their calling. This calling of leader, and pastor comes with much higher stakes, and you have to strive to make less mistakes. No one willingly signs up for this role due to the consequences and repercussions that God places on a leader going wrong are severe. So, I am baffled when I see people running to fill these positions. Through being a servant first I saw first-hand the requirements God had on my pastor, so I know I was called and sent I am not the one who went. My leader was a great leader and just coming behind her and trying to fill her shoes put a great amount of pressure on me. Although I learned from her, being out front and being "the one" was something I didn't take lightly.

I had a lot on my plate, and I wanted to protect the church, the ministry, and lead the people; all of this weighed on me because I didn't want to fell God or God's people and I wanted to protect this precious legacy that had been handed off to me unexpectedly. I knew I had to trust God even more, I had to put all of this in God's very capable hands. Coming to be a leader, the way the mantle was handed over to me made me go deeper in God, it made me have to hear from God. Just starting out in this new and very important role I wanted to first please God, and then make sure I secured the ministry and the church. I had to completely take myself out of the equation, get my hands out of God's way because things were new for me and I wanted to do a great job as a leader. I had to trust God there was no other options, I had to go into prayer and seek God for answers, I wanted to the see the ministry stay afloat and flourish there was no one to turn to except God, and He had to do it. I had to rely on His Word, in Matthew 24:35 the bible says heaven and earth shall pass away, but my words shall not pass away.

Q. Please explain the importance of leaving a legacy.

One of my legacy scriptures is taken from Philippians 4:13, I can do all things through Christ which strengthened me. This is what I want my successor to live by this is how I have learned and become an overcomer by trusting and applying God's Word to every aspect of my leadership journey and my life. It's important for me to leave a legacy so the work will continue long after God calls me home. And its' what God teaches us throughout the bible, that we should be spreading and this gospel, the good news. It's important to leave a legacy so my children, and their children can have a blueprint to follow. This is how I leave my mark on their lives, and in the world. Part of me writing this book is a tribute to my legacy, I want my children and church family to continue the work the great Bishop Ford, and great Overseer Bruce began so many years ago. And now as the mantle has been passed down to me, I want to pass the mantle down to the fourth great leader of the St. John Church of God. Who knows maybe the next leader after me will write more books, and spiritual guides for generations to come.

Q. What are the Legacy of some servant leaders you admire?

My home church that I left the pastor there was Bishop Simpson, and he was a true man of God and his legacy he left behind was love. That's what he taught us and that's what his legacy stood for, love. He stood up for and practiced righteousness, he led by example, he was a man of his word. If he said he was going to do something he did it with excellence always allowing God to lead him. A great man of God, a great pastor, a great Bishop and he just made people want to follow him in Christ. Bishop

Simpson was a father figure to all, a mentor for other ministers and leaders, he was a bible scholar he knew the Word frontwards and backwards. He loved all of his members, and he was uncompromisable!

Q. What is the legacy of the Leader you served?

What can I say about the great Overseer Sallie "Anointed" Bruce? She was just that a great woman of God. She was a no-nonsense pastor, she had this saying that still sticks out in my heart and mind today, and it's one of her favorite sayings. She'd say, "God has been good, God has been gracious, and God has been kind." Which lets me know that God has been mindful of us all, in Psalms 8:4 it says, what is man, that thou art mindful of him? And the son of man, that thou visit him? These are the things my pastor taught and lived by, she'd always say do that which is right, and sometimes you want to strike back, but I'd hear her small voice saying, "Do that which is right." Her words and commitment to God kept all of us going on the right path, she said so many important things. But she lived what she preached, talked, and sang about. She taught us to live in excellence she was a no-nonsense leader, who didn't allow half-stepping she taught us to work in excellence and go forward in God, that was her legacy.

Q. When you first became a servant leader, what did you want your legacy to be?

I want to be an overcomer. So many things come up in life, and on top of that I'm a pastor, leader, and mentor, so you must learn to be an overcomer. Life will get complicated with juggling so many roles, you will be tested, tried, and put through the fire. Also, this was one of Pastor Bruce's slogans, being an overcomer and she wanted to write a book about being an overcomer. And I believe I'm living what she wanted to write about, and this is how legacy is made just as she continued building and continuing Bishop Ford's legacy, I too am continuing building on her legacy, why because God has been good, God has been gracious, and God has been kind.

Q. What is your legacy now?

I want my legacy to be known that all I desired to do is preach the gospel, spread the good news about Jesus Christ. And that I practiced having a repented heart, before God, my desire is to continue to live a saved and sanctified life one that is pleasing to God. I want to leave a legacy that my successor will remind the followers to get their lives right with God, repent; stop playing church. Time is winding up, and God is soon to return for His people, and I want the lives that I've impacted be able to stand and cultivate their own relationship with God. The reason we must get right with God, and be ready when He appears is because His Word says no man knows the day or the hour the Son of Man shall appear, we must be ready and stay ready! In the book of Revelations chapter 22:12-14, to paraphrase; God is saying He is coming back soon, and His reward is with Him. He will pay all according to their actions on this earth, and only those who have lived according to His will can enter into the gates of Heaven. I do my best to encourage or as the Bible tells us to compel them to come in and get your hearts right with God. I would be remised if I didn't give those I've ministered to, leading or have led the opportunity to know that they must get their life right with God, we don't have as much time as we think we do. Get right with God now!

Q. Who will you pass your Mantle to?
In the book of II Kings in the second chapter, the Prophet Elijah was mentoring young Elisha, and as the story goes the Lord told Elijah that he was going to be taken up in a world wind of fire. Elijah's journey on this earth was coming to an end. As Elijah, and Elisha came to the Jordan River, Elijah took his mantle, and rolled it up and struck the waters, and the waters divided into two and they both walked across on dry land. Elijah then asked Elisha what he wanted him to do for him before he was taken away from him. Elisha requested of his Master that he wanted a double portion. Elijah said to Elisha you ask a hard thing, but if you see me at the time that I'm transitioned into heaven the double portion is for you. But if you don't see me transition into heaven the double portion isn't for you. In the Old Testament a "double portion" is likened unto a parent leaving a birthright for his first-born child. Meaning that they will have a double blessing of the legacy, or power left by a parent.
Elijah and Elisha were walking along when a fiery chariot came along and took up Elijah and separated him from Elisha and he ascended into heaven. Elisha went and picked up the mantle from his Master went back to the Jordan River, and smote the waters and it split into two, and Elisha walked across on dry land. When the waters split in two this was a confirmation that the double portion and legacy was passed to Elisha, and the bible recorded that Elisha performed more miracles than his predecessor Elijah. And as a great leader I want my successors to do more, and be greater than I was, it is the only way that my work in the ministry will prove to be effective. While I'm still waiting for God to reveal to me who my Elisha is, he or she will be more than prepared to take up the mantle or ministry and carry on as I did with my previous leader. And I

know God will allow me to see who he or she will be that is a prayer request I have before God. While I have many qualified individuals, who'd be willing to carry on and follow the blueprint that I have made and them following God, I'm confident the legacy of the St. John Church of God will continue its' work for years to come.

Q. What was the happiest/painful time of your life?
The happiest times of my life is when I received the precious gift of the Holy Ghost, got married to the love of my life, Roosevelt Brockington, Sr., and the births of my children. Also, some of the happiest times of my life was with my pastor, mentor, and friend Overseer Bruce. Other times I enjoyed helping build a ministry, serving my beloved pastor, creating businesses, and gaining revenue for the church's ministries. Traveling, spreading the gospel, and so many good times and great memories.

The most painful and difficult times of my life is the death of my son, there are no words that could describe the pain that a parent has to say good-bye to a child. It stays fresh in your mind, and my son Roosevelt, Jr. was forty years old, he was successful in life, and he had just been filled with the precious gift of the Holy Ghost, and became a deacon of the church. He was an engineer at the hospital where he worked. He had a staff that he supervised, and one of the employees didn't like the evaluation my son had given him, so the staff member took my sons life. This unexpected event affected my family deeply, including my pastor Overseer Bruce, I think it affected her more than it affected me. Because shortly after this tragic incident she suffered a stroke, she was scheduled to preach my son's eulogy, but the stroke happened. This was another very sad and difficult time in my life, and as you read in the story previously, I went through a lot to care for her during her recovery of the stroke.

During the events surrounding the death of my son, and being caretaker for my pastor, I had to attend court as the person who killed my son was standing trial. My pastor attended every day of the trial and was by me and my husband's side the whole time. There were times I couldn't take sitting in the court room listening to the events that ended my child's life, so I'd have to go out and sit in the lobby of the courts. I was so grateful for my pastor that even in her condition she was still supportive and helped us through a very difficult time in our lives. Lastly, the other most difficult time in my life is the death of my friend, mentor, and pastor. After a few years of her having health complications she passed away, and her family took me to court sighting I hadn't taken proper care of her as her caretaker. The family was giving me hard time and I had to stand trial and my ethics were questioned, this took me through a lot of difficult emotions. I had not known they were dissatisfied with my services of caring for their loved one, but she was also family to me too. But I believed God, would give me the victory in these difficult moments. I recently reunited with some of the staff where my son worked, they were honoring his memory and work at the hospital. There was a young lady a colleague of my son who wrote a letter at the Memorial for my son and it was so touching and moving. That I asked if I could share this thoughtful note as part of this book, she granted my request. This is what she wrote in memory of Roosevelt Brockington, Jr.

"Words are not always handy in the emotions of the moment. It is the day after of the memorial for your son, and I cannot stop thinking about the power of the service that took place at Suburban (Hospital) Saturday.

I was here on January 1st I saw the reactions of staff present that day, and thereafter. It was as if we lost a member of our family....even for those that did not know him or did not know him well had a guttural reaction of disbelief and pain.

It was such a deeply emotional time that I decided, to make the memorial in honor of Brock; for his department as well as staff in general....and prayed that it would give us an outlet to express our emotions, pay homage to his memory....and help us all heal.

My experience with grief is that it is helpful to be amongst those who are also grieving....and the power of the reaction of staff standing before the memorial was unbelievable....and I dare say miraculous....and beautiful. I wish that you could have witnessed the outpouring of feelings as well as meditation and prayer that the memorial evoked in so many of us. I offer you this insight not because I am the artist in this instance, I believe I was led to make this as a mere instrument for God's peace in the direction of healing from this tragedy. It was overwhelming and amazing to witness God's hand in all of this.

I experienced a tremendous loss myself just a little over a year ago. I have learned that grief is a unique journey.... deeply painful....and it forever changes us. It is something that we metabolizes in our bodies and it changes the fiber of who we are....I can say now, that my loved one gave me a tremendous gift while he was alive and an amazing gift after his death....grief walks with us every day....enriching us with greater compassion for the pain of others. Thank you for sharing your AMAZING GRACE, love and compassion with me....and your extended family here at Suburban.

And so, there were words that came to my mind in hindsight, Mom Brockington, you are AMAZING GRACE. Mother to mother I was struck by the strength of your spirit and faith....I am grateful to you and your family for sharing time with us....I dare say your son Brock truly did leave an indelible mark on all of us here....God gives us gifts to use in our lifetime, and it's up to us to use them in His honor....after watching that film of Brock during the memorial, and listening to the testimonials, it struck that there must be some measure of peace knowing your son surely used his gifts in the honor of God.
There is no doubt in my mind that both Mom and Dad Brockington were the foundation that launched Brock in His divine service.

Peace,
Marie
January 28, 2011"

Q. Please explain when you were called to be a pastor?

I couldn't say anything except yes Lord! There was nothing else left to say, but yes Lord, I'll do your will. Whatever your will is for me to do, and I still stand on that premise today, yes to the Lord. Whatever Gods' will is for my life, I accept it without any pushback. The Bible says, in the book of Acts, chapter 9: 5-6 the Lord is talking to Saul who persecuted the saints. He told Saul it is hard to kick against the pricks. But I willingly accepted the calling that God had on my life. By this time in my journey I had ideas of what God was shaping me up to be and that was to lead the

St. John Church of God, and what a great honor it has been leading God's people. But this journey is not without its share of challenges, trials, and tribulation, but I'm grateful because God says He will never leave me nor forsake me.

Q. If you could speak to the nation currently, what would be your sage advice too them?

Repent and get right with God! Do it now! Those words may seem harsh, but our souls are at stake, in I Timothy 4:6 it says, if thou put the brethren in remembrance of these things, thou shalt be a good minister of Jesus Christ. And as a minister and pastor of the gospel it my duty and well as my pleasure to put my followers or those I come into contact with in remembrance of these things. The time is now to seek God, and give your life to Him, it is the only way to eternal life, and I love preaching the gospel to those who are lost and can't seem to find peace. Jesus is the way!

Q. In your opinion is Society basically, kind or is society basically cruel?

There is cruelty in the world, but we have to look at this from a spiritual standpoint, when Satan inhabited heaven, he began to think he was more than God. (Revelation 12:7-12) He got out of his place, and foolishly believed he could overpower God, and take God's throne. A war ensued in heaven; the angels of God fought against Satan and his angels, and Satan along with his angels were cast out of heaven out into the earth. Satan prevailed NOT but was eternally forsaken by God, so when you think of the world being cruel it is. Because Satan is against good and puts cruelty in the minds of all who allow him to dwell in their thoughts. Often times the church is the target of such cruelty, the church is here to help to restore, to renew, and revive. But the church is under constant attack from the enemy and his army they are constantly finding fault, or accusing the people of God, and the church of wrongdoing. Now with that being said, are there some church leaders out there who can be and is cruel? Yes, it is, but they will have to answer to God for the mistreatment of His children. This is a why I said earlier in my story, being a pastor isn't for everyone you need to know this is very high stakes position and one should only be in this walk if they are called to do so.

If you're a pastor, and you are the "went", and not the "sent" fair warning you could be facing a harsh punishment from God, especially if you mistreat or is cruel to His people. The enemy does have processes set in place where the church is attacked, it seems as though all we do or say comes under scrutiny. But we have to remember some important facts about the war that ensued in heaven where Satan was kicked out. As he fell to the earth, he took dominion over the earth, and the earth became the place where he would set wars, confusion, attacks, and cruelty in the earth. As always God never leaves us without His promises or assurances, in John 16:33 to paraphrase God is reminding us that in Him we will have peace. In the world we will have tribulations, but He reminds us to be of good cheer because He has overcome the world. Although we may experience cruelties from the world, we shouldn't dwell on it too much because God always allows and helps us to be over comers in all that we face.

Just as there are cruel people, we see people of kindness too, I am kind to those I lead and it's important to practice kindness. A man that hath friends must show himself friendly (Proverbs 18:24), the best time to show forth acts of kindness is when you are being treated with cruelty. Hurt people; hurt people, and it's our duty as persons of God to always overcome evil with God's goodness. So, there are both cruelties, and kindness in the world, I pray that the people of God are on the right side of these two.

Conclusion

I hope you enjoyed reading my journey from how I became to be a servant to a leader. My journey wasn't linear but many ups and downs, twists and turns, challenges pushed me to the limit and along with the pressure of duty I met the challenges head on. This book is a memoir and guide to all who serve and aspire to lead a great people. The best servants and leaders are not born, but made through trials, tribulations, and hard lessons that have to be learned quickly but efficiently. When I was first called upon to volunteer with the St. John Church of God to assist the Pastor Sallie Bruce, I didn't know that God would allow this to be a more than thirty-year journey. A journey of building a legacy within a legacy, from the first Founder Bishop Ford, to Pastor Bruce, and eventually to me is a mighty story that consists of three legacies.

What was meant to be a temporary assist to an up and coming ministry turned out to be a permanent journey from servant to a thirty-year friendship to a leader. This journey is not about just the journey but a journey within journeys and then ultimately the destination. After all, why suffer through all of the strain and pressure it takes to be on a road of experience not to make it to your destination. There were times I didn't know if I'd get to the destination, and on more than one occasion the destination wasn't in plain sight. A journey and experience of this caliber isn't linear, that's where your faith must kick and be active. We didn't know some of the times what was supposed to be the next step within the journey; our most holy faith was certainly guiding us through the blind spots.

This book is relevant to audiences who can appreciate a servant's role, when I started out, I had all of the tools and or spiritual equipment to be successful in this role. I wasn't a born servant but as I continued in this journey and dedicated my heart to it, I was made an exceptional servant. Although I had all the tools and equipment within me, they had to be developed, they had to be tried, tested, and proven. Overseer Bruce had to take time to get to know me, and I had to take time to get to know her, and only a friendship/servant relationship can be successful through time. God had set His approval on this partnership, and He knew what He had in mind for this ministry, my role as servant, the growth of our friendship, and to me becoming the third successful leader of the St. John Church of God.

This book is relevant to audiences who want to learn and understand that any role you choose in life will have to take time to be developed. That is if you want to be exceptional in the role you've chosen. This issue within our culture today is that too often we don't want to cultivate or nurture our successes to full maturity, we often look at others and see their success or wealth and it looks as if they've seamlessly accomplished their success effortlessly. In Exodus 20:17, it talks about not coveting your neighbor's house, wife, ox, or servant. In paraphrasing this scripture, we look at what others have, and think it's easy to accomplish what they have accomplished. What we don't see is their journey because we are so focused on their destination. No one sees the highs and lows, the ups and downs, twists and turns, the uncertainties within the journey to getting to the destination.

This book is relevant to those who want to properly grow their businesses, whether it's corporations or a personal business. These things take time; take for example the Chinese bamboo tree takes five years to grow. You plant the seed, and the place where you plant the seed you must water and fertilize that place for at least five years. So, for the first five years you won't see any growth and the tree won't break through the ground for the first five years. With this particular tree you have to be dedicated to watering and fertilizing it for five years before you see any residuals. And servitude is just like the Chinese bamboo tree. You have to stay with it and cultivate your works, when times are hard choosing to be an over comer. When the plan of life isn't going your way and tasks are difficult or you don't have the cheering section telling you to go ahead. When you're the only one believing in your gift or dreams, and you choose to keep moving forward only in God's faith.

You keep pushing and working through it all, through the voices of the naysayers, the unbelievers, or the doubters. You find strength to keep moving forward even if it's barely or when your works are not yielding any fruit you choose to keep moving forward. Why? Because there's an innate push inside of you, that naturally propels you forward, even when you want to stop or give up you cannot. This drive is bigger than you; the over comer inside of you pushes you to keep going. But you can't stop so you keep pushing forward, it's almost as if you're on autopilot, your biggest concern is not stopping but it's to keep going. You keep going forward even though you can't see the whole journey and the destination is nowhere to be found, it's the unseen that you're moving towards, your faith is the motivator to keep going even when you don't know what's going to happen. Faith is a blind walk; faith is hindsight 2020. In Hebrews 11:6 it says, "But without faith it is impossible to please Him, for he that cometh to God must believe that He is and that He is a rewarder of them that diligently seek Him".

In Hebrews 11:1, it says "Now faith is the substance of things hoped for the evidence of things not seen." This journey as servant to a leader was a faith walk and most of it wasn't easy. It came with a lot of tests, which I had to learn quickly. I could've given up; and there were many times I wanted to. But something inside me was telling me to go ahead, and we all know what or who that something was. In Romans 8:37, it says "Yet in all these things we are more than conquerors through Him that loved us." When you choose to walk with God it will cost you many things, even your life, but God works in unorthodox ways to lose your life in God means you gain eternal life with Him in the end. To go down in God means He will bring you up, and elevate you when the time is right. Oftentimes the servant is the first one on the scene and the last to leave, our work isn't always appreciated. There's a stigma associated with being a servant, we're persons to be looked down upon, to be talked to in any kind of way, to be demanded by those who feel they're better than us. Oftentimes we're treated as slaves.

Earlier in my conclusion I began giving an analogy about the Chinese bamboo tree, how it has to be watered and fertilized for at least five years before the tree breaks through the ground. And I like this analogy to my story as a servant to becoming a leader. It took many years of hard work cultivating my relationships with many people; some was only in my life long enough for me to learn a lesson. While others had a more permanent position in my journey. But after years of working hard, putting in long hours, seeking God, going through different seasons with people, changes, and challenges I began to see progress in my journey. And once you break through that ground and find your spiritual rhythm things can move very quickly so I had to pay close attention to what God was saying and have me do it.

After you've fertilized and watered a Chinese bamboo tree for five years, the tree breaks through the ground. After it breaks through the ground, within five months it can grow up to more than ninety feet tall. So you can visibly see this tree growing before your eyes daily, and this is how our God works. The journey could get off to a rough start and you may not understand how things are going to work out. But stay and work, build, cultivate your dreams. Keep watering those ideas, keep fertilizing the work plant a seed, give God something to bless and increase. Be an over comer; don't give up on what your dreams are. If you do you won't be able to see how quickly God will increase your gifts in five months like the Chinese bamboo tree. Now the math may be different for some, but the point I am making is that nothing is gained without you persevering, staying and being committed. Give God something to work with, you must give God something to bless or increase and that is where your faith comes in.

This isn't just about my story, but this book is for all who wants to know and understand what it takes to build a ministry from the ground up, and then maintain what God has allowed you to build. This book is for new pastors that need to be encouraged and give up on your journey as a new leader. This is for the first ladies/man who needs a guide to understanding how to support your husband/wife in their leadership journey as they're starting out as pastors/leaders. This is a book for the entrepreneur who is attempting to find their way to start their dreams and turning their dreams into a business. This book is for the CEO of a fortune 500 company they too can learn from my experience as being a successful leader to many people that were under my tutelage. This book is for the small business owner, in my story you'll read how I had to be innovative and take calculated risks to have a successful ministry/business.

In my conclusion I feel this book is for all people, with diverse backgrounds, cultures, and even religious beliefs. All can find something useful in my story that will encourage you to be an over comer as I was. To break through all barriers and overtake any challenge that threatened to stifle my successes as servant or leader. In this book you will read about how a common purpose threaded over thirty years, three leaders, had built ministries, businesses, and communities. But none of this would've been possible without God, and each person having strong faith that all things could be accomplished through God. In Romans 8:18, it says "For I reckon that the sufferings of this present time are not worthy to be compared with the glory which shall be revealed in us." If you stick with what God wants you to do, I promise you that after a while just like that Chinese bamboo tree, after a few years of hard work that tree sprang forth fruit in a few months. Our hard work is always quickly multiplied by God's rewards if you go through and don't lose faith or stop working. God will increase and bless what you have planted.

A PICTORIAL OF SERVITUDE

BISHOP JESSE FORD
FOUNDER

Overseer Dr. Sallie A. Bruce

"God has been Good! God has been Gracious! and
God has been Kind!"

Happy Twentieth Pastoral Anniversary
to our Pastor

Dr. Sallie A. Bruce

St. John Ford Memorial
Church of God Inc.
1301 H Street, NE
Washington, DC 20002

Happy 24th

Pastoral Anniversary

To Our Pastor

Overseer, Sallie A. Bruce

Happy 27th
Pastoral Anniversary

Overseer Sallie A. Bruce
May 27, 2012
5:00 pm

A Chapter From "The Book of Bruce"

The writer has taken the liberty to delve into a long-awaited enterprise that of the authentic writing of life's journey according to Overseer Bruce.

Being mindful, such an extraordinary manuscript can only be effectuated by the mind, body, and soul of our distinguished Honoree, being celebrated today.

Please allow me to indulge myself as I attempt to interpret what I see and at the same time; ask you, her captive audience, "What Are You Looking At"?

Can you look beyond her "temporary physical limitations"? We cannot negate the fact that several catastrophic events unfolded, causing a set-back in the physical aspect, but more importantly an astonishing bounce-back in her spirit. All praises be to God Almighty.

Last year in review, coupled with this year's heartbreaking events have been a time of turbulence for the "Anointed" one. Something's we know, and then there are occurrences we don't need to know. Is that alright? The end results are matters of importance. God alone will be continuously praised for his mighty acts and wondrous works. There is no stopping this warrior. She knows through suffering that great triumphs are borne out of great troubles.

When Overseer returned to her pulpit on the 1st Sunday in March of this year, we witnessed her tenacity and fearless manner. Guess what else we saw?

- *Her Faith - Astonishingly secure*
- *Love - Unblemished*
- *Hope - Enough to last a lifetime*
- *Patience - Unlimited and powerful*
- *Mind -Intact! She has the mind of Christ, Satan you can't touch this.*
- *Gifts - Still in operation, extraordinarily so*
- *Vision - Elevated beyond measurer in fact taken to another level*
- *Belief - Unshaken*

The wonder of it all, God yet abides within and is still at work in this vessel, not patching, but making new. The best of the rest is soon to come. Her attitude towards and approach to hardship has enabled her to overcome many, many obstacles. She has learned to accept what God allows.

Her will to press onward in spite of, brings added assurance that God is her rock, and that he has always been a shelter in the time of storms. We notify the devil today that you can see her, but can't come where she is - safe in the hands of Jesus, be assured it is well with her soul.

Lastly, the question is - if someone would read your life like a book, will they find Jesus in the pages?

Please, let us stand all over this building and give God a "Standing Ovation" for the life of our beloved Overseer and friend, Dr. Sallie "Anointed' Bruce.

Written By: Mother Gwendolyn Kennedy

Celebrating the Lifi e of
Overseer Dr. Sallie (Anointed) Bruce

Overseer Sallie A. Bruce

"God has been Good! God has been Gracious! and God has been Kind!

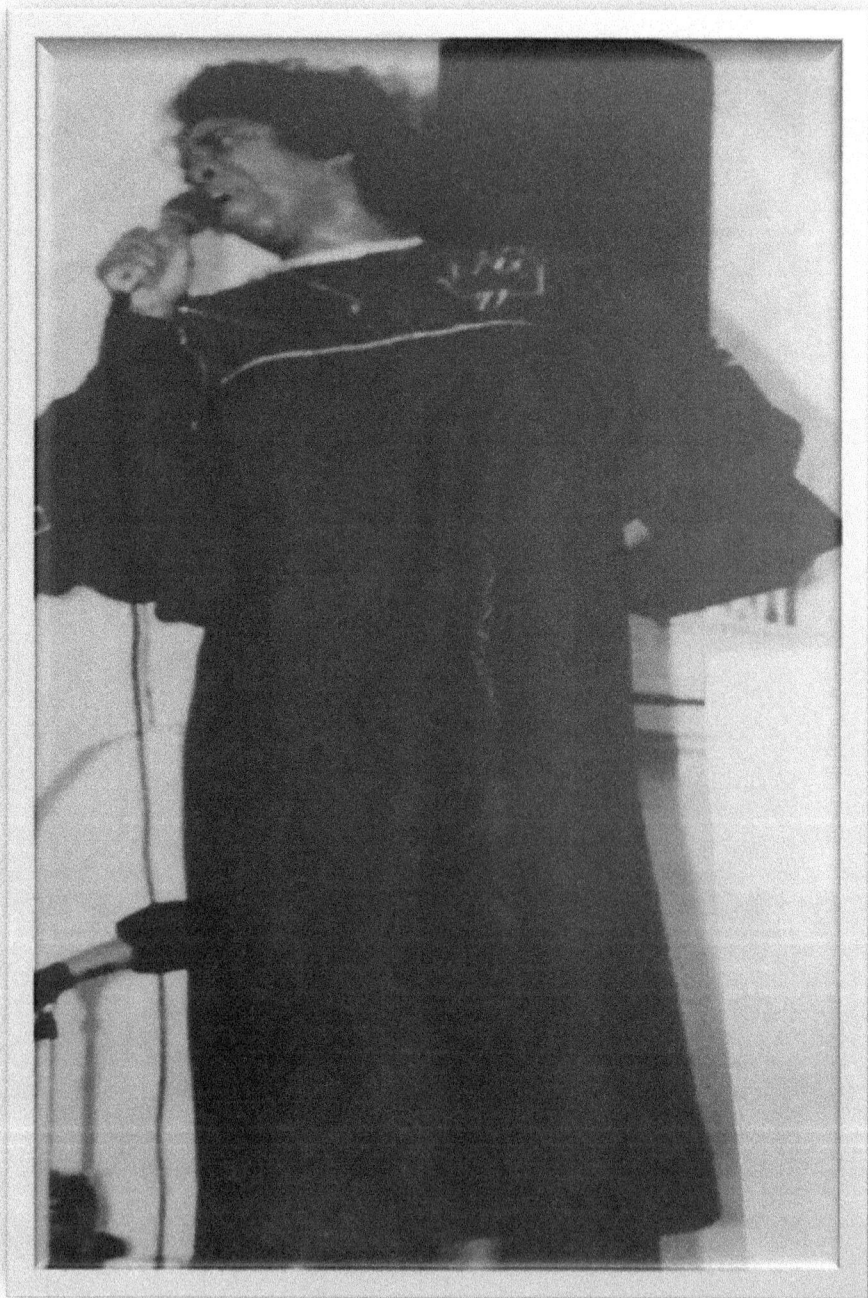

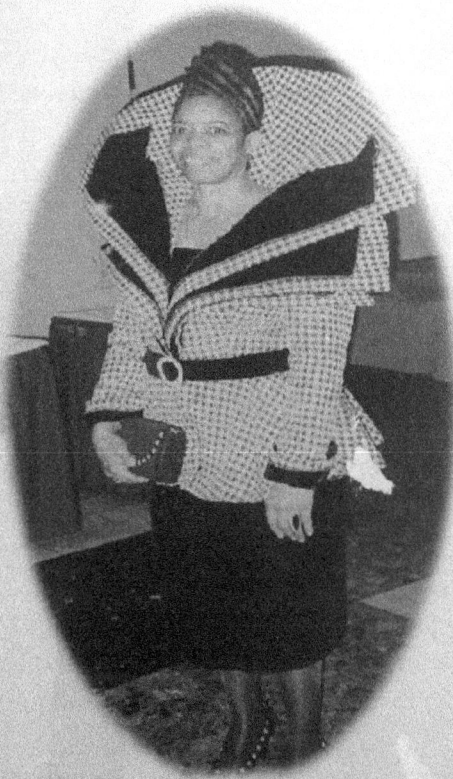

"It Can Be Done"

25th Pastoral Anniversary
Overseer Dr. Sallie A. L...

The Announcer Speaks

I would like to take this opportunity to share with you just what I mean when I introduce my "Pastor", Dr. Sallie A. Bruce

Introduction

It is my "Honor" today – Respect you, Esteem you highly.

As well as it is a "Privilege" – A special advantage or benefit granted to me and enjoyed by me.

To bring to you – To Introduce to you

Our "Pastor" – Pastor after God's own heart.

The Woman of God of the "Hour" – For this specified period of time.

Women of God with the "Message" – there is always a fresh word from the Lord.

Women of God that's standing on the wall – Standing Tall not taking down for anything, when you have done all to stand she stands anyhow.

Crying Loud – Crying Loud against sin speaking plain and clear so that nobody has any excuses.

Sparing Not – Preaching in Season & out of season, not worrying whether we like it or not.

Lifting up her voice like a trumpet in Zion – Taking this gospel everywhere it can go thru radio, television and Revivals.

Telling dying men and women everywhere that Christ is the answer.

Woman of God that "Loves God" with all her heart, unconditional Love.

"Trust God" – She believes that God can turn things around no matter how it looks.

"Obeys God" – Doing the will of God wanting to be in his perfect will.

Women with a Prophetic Ministry – women who speaks by divine inspiration having the Nature of Prophesy.

None other than Dr. Sallie Anointed Bruce – The spirit of the Lord uses her in a mighty way.

Reverend Paulette Brockington

Touch By An Angel

To My Pastor,
Dr. Sallie A. Bruce

I wanted to take this time to congratulate you on 28 years of Pastoring the Greatest Church in all the world because you are the Greatest Pastor in all the world.

I thank God for you everyday for your stand in God in your Life you are my mentor, you have set an example for me and anyone else that will follow. I hear the saying all the time about everybody has an angel. Well I believe that because you are my Angel. Pastor you really are an inspiration to everyone you come in contact with, you are just you. And like you say all the time your life is an open book "God has smiled on you" I want to say that I have been Touch by an Angel, which is you!

I thank God for all your accomplishment in ministry, you came from Minister Bruce, Pastor Bruce, Dr. Bruce and now Overseer Bruce. Started Radio Ministry, TV Ministry, in 49 cities across the country. Recorded two CD's purchase, TV equipment, rebuilt the ministry needed to move forward, you took us to the next level. Remembered your calling me an morning and told me to pick you up. You were going to purchase a bus for church as usual I did not question you. I did what I was told and picked you up and preceded to the bus company. We met with the salesman and you told him what you wanted. He in return question you, Reverend how much money do you have to put down, you looked at me and turned to him and said. I do not have any money. He said Reverend how are you going to get this bus. Pastor stated "You are going to order it and you are", we willing do this and you will do that and he did. Two months later we received a call that the bus was in sent from the manufacture, and they ask how she wanted the writing on her bus. See what the Lord has done.

The Lord Bless you with one daycare, then there was St. John Kiddie Kollege II, and now St. John Kiddie Kollege III on the move. After all of this God has increase your vision. You are in the process of building God a new edifice.

T - *Taught me how to <u>Trust God in all things</u>*

O - *Be obedient to the <u>will</u> of <u>God</u> and <u>leadership</u>*

U - *<u>Understand</u> even when you <u>don't</u> want to <u>understand</u>*

C - *Ask God for a <u>Clean Heart</u> and renew the right spirit in us*

H - *You taught us its <u>Holiness</u> or <u>Hell</u> theirs no other way.*

E - *Eger and Eveready to do what I can do for ministry*

D – *Declaring the <u>Gospel of Jesus Christ</u> in season and out of season.*

B - *Believing God for everything building, Ministry*

Y - *Just say <u>Yes</u> to the <u>Lord</u>*

A - *An <u>all</u> thy why <u>acknowledge</u> him he will direct your path*

N - *Never give up the Lord is on our side*

A - *<u>Anointed</u> I can't do anything without the anointing*

N – *<u>Need</u> always realize that I need more of God in my Life*

G - *<u>Give</u> all of <u>you</u>, your <u>time</u>, <u>finances</u> to God and ministry*

E - *<u>Encourage</u>, you have keep me encourage through you <u>Stand</u> with God*

L - *Love lifted me, you have shown Love and given Love with Loving Kindness you have drawn me*

With Love
You are my Touched Angel
Assistant Pastor Paulette Brockington

Dr. Sallie A. Bruce:
We would like to offer our heartfelt congratulations on this 25th momentous occasion. Giving of one's self in service is among the highest expressions of caring and God's love. You are to be deeply thanked for having given of yourself so freely for so long to the members of your congregation and to the people around the World.
Affectionately,
The True Deliverance Church of Jesus Christ Family
Honorable Pastor ~ Dr. Madiean Colter
2445 West Washington Street
Phoenix, Arizona 85009
"Small but Mighty in God"

"If I Were Here Today"

If I were here today I would be so excited, checking and double-checking every detail to the letter. It was of the utmost importance to me that nothing was withheld, but everything given to make these occasions "grand affairs." Everything had to be beautiful and in order.

If I were here today, I'd be applauding wildly and yes smiling to keep back tears of joy that would whelm up in my eyes.

If I were here today, I would once again experience the pride and admiration that never failed to engulf me. As I watched you work the crowd, flashing that dazzling smile in acknowledgment and acceptance of their love, I would say "That's My Pastor."

Well, I'm not here today, but yet everything is in place. No stone has been left unturned. Those that have been entrusted down through the years are in place and have stepped up the pace. They will assure you without me that the latter celebrations of your Anniversaries will be greater than those passed.

Loving You Always,
Deacon Roosevelt Brockington, Jr.

Written By: Mother Gwendolyn Kennedy

Celebration of Life
for
Deacon Roosevelt Brockington, Jr.
July 12, 1970 – January 1, 2011

Saturday, January 8, 2011
Viewing: 9:00 a.m.- 11:00 a.m.
Services: 11:00 a.m.

New Horizon Christian Faith Church
2211 Varnum Street
Mt. Rainier, Maryland 20712
Dr. Charlene Monk
Officiating: Overseer, Dr. Sallie A. Bruce
St. John Ford Memorial Church of God

Special Moments

50th
Wedding Anniversary Ceremony

Roosevelt Sr. & Paulette Brockington

Sunday, The Fourth of August 2013

At Two O'clock In The Afternoon

Camelot of Upper Marlboro
13901 Central Avenue
Upper Marlboro, Maryland 20774

Homegoing Service

for

Anthony I. Bruce

Wednesday, December 3, 1997
11:00 A.M.

t. John Ford Memorial Church of God
1301 "H" Street, Northeast
Washington, DC 20002

Doctor Sallie A. Bruce - Pastor
Bishop Harold J. Benjamin - Eulogist
Elder George Davis - Officiating

Anthony I. Bruce

"Little Man"

1961 - 1997

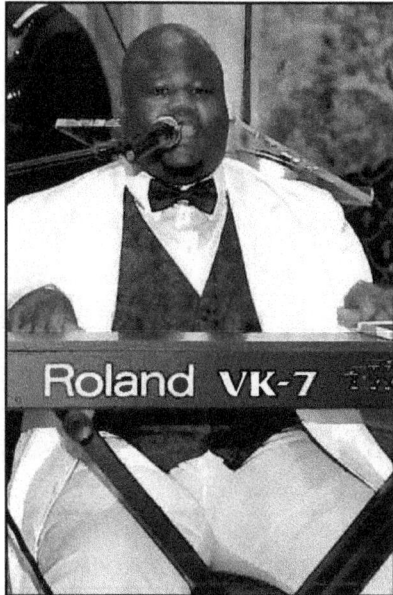

My Journey as A Servant

Who's Who In The City

Heroes, Heroines and Champions Among Us

Welcome to

Who's Who In The City

Founded, Produced and Hosted

by

Reverend Paulette Brockington

Welcome to Rev. Paulette Brockington's forum.

Seeking and presenting champions who live, work and serve amongst us. Those that labor without any thought of recompense. The reward of a job well done, a sermon well delivered, a song soulfully sung and a tenacious spirit in the face of opposition are compensation enough.

Paulette Brockington

Overseer Sallie A. Bruce

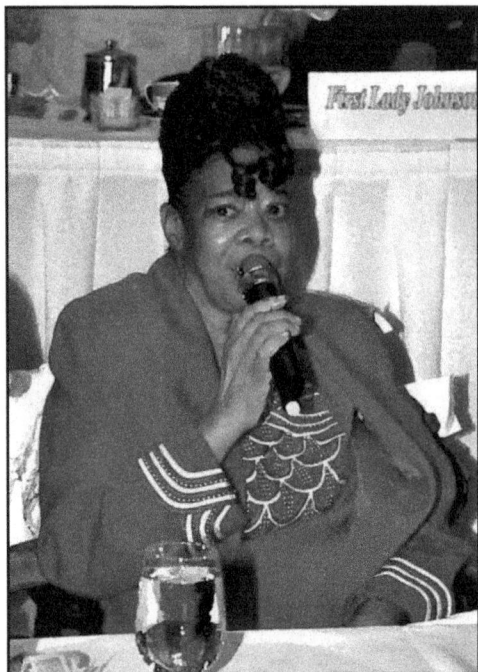

An Unknown Destiny

Who would have thought, Who would have imagined, and it is assured not this woman of whom this true exposition is about. It is not often that one gets to tribualize one

while they live, but for me it is a pleasure that I hold dearly.

It all began in a little storefront church under the guidence and tutoring of the late Dr. Jessie Ford. It was not in any

sense that it would come a time that this woman would later

become the Chief Shepherd. For her, it began in the Sunday

school where she was merely a listenner, a learner, a worker,

then a teacher. Moreover, she is not the type of person that

wanted to be highlighted for she knew her place and represented it well. But, it was always known even by her

leader, along with others that constantly observed her that she

had an unknown destiny. The destiny to lead within the church

with an anointing placed upon her by God.The destiny became

a reality one day, one year, and, a season chosen by God when

that anointing and calling was to be enacted. As like all other

②

biblical representatives that have gone before her, it was not in

her vision that she would be placed in a position to lead. But,

when that day, that year, that time, and, that season came,

she heard the voice of the Lord say Take Up the Charge My

Anointed One. She not only became the Chief
Shephered, she became Dr. Sallie Anointed Bruce.

This anointing and calling would take her many places

throughout the christian world by way of tleevision, radio, and,

personal appearences through revivals and various crusades.

Yes, Dr. Sallie Anointed Bruce, I am writing about you.

You who I have worked, fellowship with, and, observed.

A Destiny Unknown now has become fulfilled with the promise of
God. I sayto you continue on as you celebrate twenty-five

year anniversy, simply because it began in the Sunday school.

It is not often that one enters into there destiny without
prior preparation. But, Sallie, your entrence into
your destiny was quiet, silent, but already prepared.

Bishop John L. Taylor

Paulette

P- Is for the pride St. John have in you.

A- Is for always-you are always doing for someone else you never stop to think of yourself.

U- Is for uses-you let God uses you in every way, whether its night or day.

L- Is for love -you spread love all over the nation, you show love in all situation.

E- Is for excited- you get excited when you talking about the Lord, you let everyone know he is first in your life. But you also light up,let everyone know you are Decon Brockington wife.

T- Is for test- you did your homework you passed all the tests Rev & TV Producer you are the best.

T- Is for tired- you never get tired working for the Lord, you are a warrior that stand tall on the ground. Oh yes the Lord going to give you your crown.

E- Is for end- this is not the end for you, this is only the begining I'll close now and thank God for you Amen.

By: Mother Martha Stewart

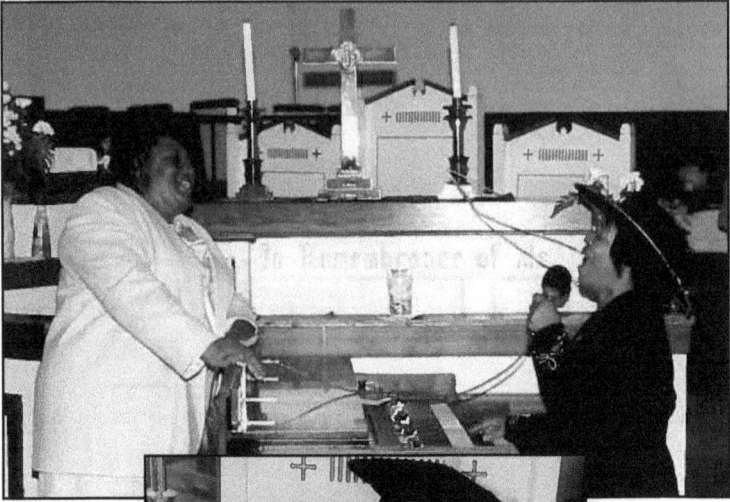

The Very Pastor Paulette Brockington

Wife, Mother, Grandmother, Friend, **Pastor of St. John Church of God,** **Servant,** Confidant, **God's Choice,** Selfless, **Jeremiah 1:5,** Serious, Compassionate, Anointed, Business Owner, Brave, Strong, Lender, Giver, Accomplished, **Overcomer,** Hebrews 13:5, Firm, **Straightforward,** God Fearing, God Pleaser, **Bold, Beautiful,** Caring, Leader, **Numbers 23:19-20,** Administrator, Loyal, **Trustworthy,** Kind, Great Preacher, Teacher, Jeremiah 29:11, **Bible Believer,** Director, Restaurant Owner, **Hebrews 11:1,** Integrity, Fiduciary, Awesome, Kindhearted, Tender, Happy, Chauffeur, Proverbs 31 Woman, Faithful, Outgoing, Gracious, Peacemaker, Isaiah 49:16, Fervent, **Driven,** Gentle, Fearless, Entrepreneur, **Book Author,** Mentor, Philanthropist, Focused, **Dedicated,** Perseverance, Hard Worker, Brilliant, Ordinary, Extraordinary, Noble, **Psalm 27:14,** Zealous, Warmhearted, **Honorable,** Doer, Supportive, Audacious, Enchanting, **Mighty Woman of God,** Outstanding, Innovative, Resilient, **Unique,** Super Special, **Courageous,** Insightful, Enthusiastic, **II Chronicles 7:14,** Sympathetic, Woman with a Plan, Sensitive, Confident, Delightful, Psalm 27:1,   She's our Paulette, Mind- Blowing, Genuine, **Passionate,** Hebrews 11:6, Determined, Eager, Fervent, Knowledgeable, Sincere, Ambitious, Putting other First, Psalm 139:14, Powerful, **Extraordinary,** First Rated, Composer, Lovely, Esther 4:14, Hero, Yes she can!, Amiable, Leave it to me, **Caring, Philippians 4:13,** I can handle this, Willing, Contemplative, Tough, World Traveler, Inspired, Confidant, Renowned, Sought After, Devoted, Gutsy, Exceptional, Zechariah 2:8, **Queen,** Contributor, Intentional, Hero, Committed, Wise, Conqueror, Warm, Positive, Gentle, Giant, Achiever, Woman of Action, **Matthew 6:33,** Motivated, Simple, Resourceful, Trailblazer, Phenomenal, Songstress, Dependable, Chosen.

The Very Pastor Paulette Brockington,

You're Simply the BEST!

We love you, Joyce Plaisival & Kimberly Colter –Phoenix, Arizon

My Journey as A Servant

www.ingramcontent.com/pod-product-compliance
Lightning Source LLC
Chambersburg PA
CBHW032012040426
42448CB00006B/606